T0077877

THE
GREAT PHYSICIAN
FOR
COVID-19

ROY DIXON

authorHOUSE·

AuthorHouse™
1663 Liberty Drive
Bloomington, IN 47403
www.authorhouse.com
Phone: 833-262-8899

Published by AuthorHouse 07/16/2020

ISBN: 978-1-7283-6065-2 (sc)
ISBN: 978-1-7283-6064-5 (e)

Print information available on the last page.

*Any people depicted in stock imagery provided by Getty Images are models,
and such images are being used for illustrative purposes only.
Certain stock imagery © Getty Images.*

This book is printed on acid-free paper.

*Because of the dynamic nature of the Internet, any web addresses or
links contained in this book may have changed since publication and
may no longer be valid. The views expressed in this work are solely those
of the author and do not necessarily reflect the views of the publisher,
and the publisher hereby disclaims any responsibility for them.*

KJV
*Scripture quotations marked KJV are from the Holy Bible, King James
Version (Authorized Version). First published in 1611. Quoted from the KJV
Classic Reference Bible, Copyright © 1983 by The Zondervan Corporation.*

CONTENTS

THE GREAT PHYSICIAN FOR COVID-19

And said, If thou wilt diligently hearken to the voice of the LORD thy God, and wilt do that which is right in his sight, and wilt give ear to his commandments, and keep all his statutes, I will put none of these diseases upon thee, which I have brought upon the Egyptians: for I am the LORD that healeth thee. [Exodus 15:26]

If my people who are called by My name will humble themselves, and pray and seek My face, and turn from their wicked ways, then I will hear from heaven, and will forgive their sin, and will heal their land. [2 Chronicles 7:14]

If the reader is infected with the COVID-19 virus and desire to be heal, I encourage the reader to pray this simple prayer and believe in your heart that you are going to be healed. If you are unable to talk, just meditate on this prayer and believe and don't doubt!

PRAYER PRESCRIPTION FOR COVID-19

"Oh Jehovah-Rapha, the Great Physician, "I accept you as my Lord and Saviour, I repent of all my sins, I accept your blood atonement that was shed for me at Calvary. I place my faith in your Divine healing, by your stripes I am healed, and I rebuke this virus and claim my healing in the name of the Lord Jesus Christ!"

I shall not die, but live, and declare the works of the LORD. [Psalms 118:17]

This book is dedicated to an elect group of people around the world who are looking for answers to the Coronavirus.

The scribe is Roy Dixon but the Author is the Lord Jesus Christ. The prescription for the COVID-19 virus listed in this book is not fiction but only a few people will choose to take the prescription from the Great Physician and accept His Divine healing.

ROY DIXON

COMFORTING SCRIPTURES TO ALLEVIATE THE CORONAVIRUS NEUROSIS

Comfort ye, comfort ye my people, saith your God Speak ye comfortably to Jerusalem, and cry unto her, that her warfare is accomplished, that her iniquity is pardoned: for she hath received of the LORD's hand double for all her sins. The voice of him that crieth in the wilderness, Prepare ye the way of the LORD, make straight in the desert a highway for our God. Every valley shall be exalted, and every mountain and hill shall be made low: and the crooked shall be made straight, and the rough places plain: And the glory of the LORD shall be revealed, and all flesh shall see it together: for the mouth of the LORD hath spoken it. The voice said, Cry. And he said, What shall I cry? All flesh is grass, and all the goodliness thereof is as the flower of the field. The grass withereth, the flower fadeth: because the spirit of the LORD bloweth upon it: surely the people is grass. [Isaiah 40:1-8] There shall no evil befall thee, neither shall any plague come nigh thy dwelling. [Psalms 91:10]

Heal me, OLORD, and I shall be healed; save me, and I shall be saved: for thou art my praise. [Jeremiah 17:14] Come unto me, all ye that labour and are heavy laden, and I will give you rest. Take my yoke upon you, and learn of me; for I am meek and lowly in heart: and ye shall find rest unto your souls. [Matthew 11:28-29]. Peace I leave with you, my peace I give unto you: not as the world giveth, give I unto you. Let not your heart be troubled, neither let it be afraid. [John 14:27] Fear thou not; for I am with thee: be not dismayed; for I am thy God: I will strengthen thee; yea, I will help thee; yea I will uphold thee with the right hand of my righteousness. [Isaiah 41:10] For God hath not given us the spirit of fear, but of power, and of love and of a sound mind. 2 Timothy 1:7]

CHAPTER 1

CORONAVIRUS ("COVID-19")

Quotations from the World Health Organization: The Coronavirus was first detected in China and has now been characterized as a global pandemic. The virus has been named "SARS-CoV-2" and the disease it causes has been named "Coronavirus disease 2019" (abbreviated "COVID-19"). Pandemics happen when a new virus emerges to infect people and can spread between people sustainably. Because there is little to no pre-existing immunity against the new virus, it spreads worldwide"."On January 30, 2020, the International Health Regulations Emergency Committee of the World Health Organization (WHO) declared the outbreak a "public health emergency" of international concern. On January 31, 2020 Health and Human Services Secretary declared a public health emergency (PHE) for the United States to aid the nation's healthcare community in responding to COVID-19. "On March 11, 2020 the World

Health Organization publicly characterized COVID-19 as a pandemic." "It may be possible that a person can get COVID-19 by touching a surface or object that has the virus on it and then touching their own mouth, nose, or possibly their eyes, but this is not thought to be the main way the virus spreads. For most patients, COVID-19 begins and ends in the lungs, because like the flu, Coronaviruses are respiratory diseases." They spread typically when an infected person coughs or sneezes, spraying droplets that can transmit the virus to anyone in close contact. Coronaviruses also cause flu-like symptoms: patients might start out with a fever and cough that progresses to pneumonia or worse. After the SARS outbreak, the World Health Organization reported that the disease typically attacked the lungs in three phases: viral replication, immune hyper-reactivity, and pulmonary destruction.

"In the early days of an infection, the novel Coronavirus rapidly invades human lung cells. Those lung cells come in two classes: ones that make mucus and ones with hair-like batons called cilia". "Mucus, though gross when outside the body, helps protect lung tissue from pathogens and make sure your breathing organ doesn't dry out. The cilia cells beat around the mucus, clearing out debris like pollen or viruses. SARS loved to infect and kill cilia cells, which then sloughed off and filled patients' airways with debris and fluids, and hypothesizes that the same is happening with the novel Coronavirus. That's because the earliest studies on COVID-19 have shown that many patients develop pneumonia in both lungs, accompanied by symptoms like shortness of breath. That's when phase two and the immune system kicks in. Aroused by the presence of a viral invader, our bodies step up to fight the disease by flooding the lungs with immune cells to clear away the damage and repair the lung tissue." When working properly, this inflammatory process is tightly regulated and confined only to infected areas. But sometimes your immune system goes haywire and those cells kill anything in their way, including your healthy tissue. During the third phase, lung damage continues to build—which can result in respiratory failure. Even if death doesn't occur, some patients survive with permanent lung damage.

According to the WHO, SARS punched holes in the lungs, giving them "a honeycomb-like appearance"— and these lesions are present in those afflicted by novel Coronavirus, too." "These holes are likely created by the immune system's hyperactive response, which creates scars that both protect and stiffen the lungs. When that occurs, patients often have to be put on ventilators to assist their breathing." "Meanwhile, inflammation also makes the membranes between the air sacs and blood vessels more permeable, which can fill the lungs with fluid and affect their ability to oxygenate blood. In severe cases, your lungs are fill with fluid and you can't breathe and that's how people are dying." Pharmaceutical scientists around the world are scrambling to develop a vaccine for the virus. There is a remedy for the COVID-19 virus but the world refuses to acknowledge and turn to the person who have the prescription, the Great Physician.

CHAPTER 2

THE DREAM

The world has been applying an ancient Biblical remedy to stop the spread of the COVID-19 virus. Government leaders around the world issued mandates for people to stay in their homes to quarantine for 14 days to prevent the spread of the virus. In the ancient times they had to quarantine a lamb for 14 days and then killed the lamb on the fourteen day and put the blood upon the side door posts and the upper door post for a Token in order to be protected from the plague of death.

The Coronavirus plague outbreak has killed thousands of people and has paralyzed the entire world financial system. It has caused Global stocks to plummet and has shut down the world economy system such as, the entertainment industries, colleges, schools, churches, synagogues, mosques, hotels, cruise ships, airports, auto plants, restaurants, et certera. The COVID-19 pandemic outbreak has taken a hold on the Global economy. Scientists around the world are scrambling to develop a vaccine for the Coronavirus and are experimenting with blood plasma antibodies from people who has recovered from the virus. 1900 years ago a cure was found for all diseases and sickness in blood plasma antibodies of the Great Physician. He donated His blood to save the world from the original disease and provided an inoculation that is free of charge.

In January 2020 William went to Wuhan China on a business trip for his job and when he returned to the United States, he discovered he was infected with the Coronavirus and had to be admitted into the hospital for shortness of breath and a high fever. After one month William was released from the hospital and allowed to go home. When he came home from the hospital, he checked his voice messages and his employer had called and left a message advising him that he was laid off from work due to Covid-19.

In June 2020 William was running out of money and food and prayed to the Lord to send someone to his home with some food. William asked the Lord to help world leaders to find a vaccine for the Covid-19 virus and fell asleep. He dreamed a man clothed in white linen came to his home and knocked on his door and said he was thirsty and hungry and asked for something to drink and eat. William told the stranger he had been laid off from his job and only had a little food left for himself. The stranger pleaded for a glass of water and for something to eat. William felt compassion for the stranger and invited him into his home to give him something to drink and eat. When William opened his refrigerator door to get the stranger a glass of water, he was astonish to find his refrigerator was full of food. When William opened his pantry to get some bread to fix the stranger a sandwich, his pantry was full of food. The dream scene changed and they were translated to a distant land. When they arrived in the distant land many young people in their early twenties wearing white linen clothing came running to greet William.

The man clothed in linen asked William, "do you recognize any of the young people?" and he stated, "No". The man clothed in linen said, "they are the saints who died on earth and their spirits ascended to this six dimension to their celestial bodies. For we know that if our earthly house [body] of this tabernacle were dissolved [die], we have a building of God, an house [celestial body] not made with hands [not born of a woman], eternal in the heavens. For in this we groan, earnestly desiring to be clothed upon with our house which is from heaven: If so be that being clothed we shall not be found naked. For we that are in this tabernacle do groan, being burdened: not for that we would be unclothed, but clothed upon, that mortality might be swallowed up of life. [2 Corinthians 5:1-4]

CHAPTER 3

THE BEGINNING

The man clothed in linen said to William, "There is a natural body and there is a spiritual body. You were born on earth through your mother in a natural body in flesh and blood bearing a spirit, you bypassed your heavenly body for a specific purpose of the LORD God Almighty.

As is the earthy, such are they also that are earthy: and as is the heavenly, such are they also that are heavenly. And as we have borne the image of the earthy, we shall also bear the image of the heavenly. Now this I say, brethren, that flesh and blood cannot inherit the kingdom of God; neither doth corruption inherit incorruption. Behold, I shew you a mystery; We shall not all sleep, but we shall all be changed, In a moment, in the twinkling of an eye, at the last trump: For the trumpet shall sound, and the dead shall be raised incorruptible, and we shall be changed. For this corruptible must put on incorruption, and this mortal must put on immortality. [1 Corinthians 15:48-53]

"When the last trump shall sound, Christ will return to earth and rapture His saints, they will meet the Lord Jesus in the sky for the Wedding Feast to bear their celestial bodies, and the earthly veils will be lifted and their heavenly conscious will be restored to know all things from the beginning. The man clothed in linen said, "human beings bypassed their celestial bodies [Theophany bodies] and were born on earth in flesh and spirit through a woman to be tried and proven by God for His redemption story."

"The different bewteen human beings and Christ, He was born with His Theophany, [celestial body] that is the reason He knew all things from the beginning of the world. The human beings are not conscious of all things from the beginning because they bypassed their celestial bodies and were born in their telestial bodies in flesh and blood. The LORD Almighty placed earthly veils upon their eyes to blind them of their celestial consicous of those things that happen with Him in the beginning in the unseen spiritual world. They are veiled to their celestial conscious that they were sons and dauthers of God who were born from the Spirit of God and resisted the devil's lies when he accused them before God in the spiritual world."

"Adam was the only person born with his celestial body on earth and the LORD God took his celestial body back after he fell in sin to protect the woman. After the fall every human being had to bypassed their celestial body and were born in a telestial body on earth." The man clothed in linen said to William, " In the beginning before there ever was a star, planet, moon or anything, there was nothing but space, no atoms, no air, no light but darkness and a great fountain of Spirit that covered all the universe. This great fountain of all Eternity was full of love, power, joy, wisdom, knowledge, peace, righteousness, holiness, honesty, et certera, and was and is the river of life. This great fountain of Spirit was the Father of Glory, the Great fountain of all Eternity." "In the Beginning the Father of Glory spoke from this great fountain of Eternity which fills all space and said, "Let there be light: and out of this great fountain of Spirit was a loud "Thunder", the "Big Bang". The mystery to this "Big Bang" is that the "Spirit of God" gave birth to Himself, as the only begotten Son of God in the Beginning before there every was an atom. "Out of this Great Thunder came the VOICE OF GOD, which was the Son of God that appeared as a Supernatural little Halo of light that shone in all the universe. This Supernatural Halo of Light was the Logos, the living Word of God that formed into the image of a Theophany; Supernatural celestial heavenly body, which was the beginning of the creation of God. [Genesis 1:3]

"In the beginning was the Word, and the Word was with God, and the Word was God. The same was in the beginning with God. All things were made by Him; and without Him was not anything made that was made." [John 1:1-14] [Revelation 3:14] The Son of God was the only visible form of the great fountain of Spirit that became visible as a pillar of light. That is why Jesus said, "and now O Father, glorify thou me with thine own self with the glory which I had with thee before the world was." [John 17:5] No man hath seen God at any time; the only begotten Son, which is in the bosom of the Father, he hath declared him. [John 1:18] "This Supernatural Halo of light called the Logos, pillar of fire or Theophany, was the first manifestation of the living Word of God that was Spoken out of the existence of the great fountain of Spirit, which is, and which was, and which is to come, the Almighty.

"It was the great celestial Body of Jehovah God that formed into an image of a Supernatural Halo of Light, out of which all visible forms of life were created. This Theophany of the Son of God was made flesh in the person of the Lord Jesus Christ." The man clothed in linen said, "Man was born from that Supernatural Halo of light in the Beginning when God said, "Let us make man in our image, after our likeness. God created man as angelic beings in the beginning, they rotated off the Supernatural Halo of light and were created as celestial bodies from the "SPIRIT of God." They appeared as morning Stars and sons of God but they are not conscious of their celestial bodies because of their earthly veils. "Jesus told His disciples that He knew them before the foundation of the world. He told Jeremiah, "before I formed you in the womb I knew you, before you were born I sanctified you; I ordained you a prophet to the nations." [Jeremiah 1:5] Where were you when I laid the foundation of the earth? Tell me if you understand. When the morning stars sang together, and all the sons of God shouted for joy? [Job 38:4,7] "The Son of God, the Logos started playing around creating the planets in the galaxy like a little child in all Eternity and all the sons of God shouted for joy at His Majestic and creativity. The Son of God said, "Let there be lights in the heavens to divide the day from the night and let them be for signs and for seasons, and for days and years." [Genesis 1:14-16]

"First He create the sun, He said, "Let there be Light, and when He did, an atom burst and the sun came into existence. The sun whirled for hundreds of millions of years burning and breaking atoms and then a big clinker fell off of the sun about the size of the earth. "He let it fall for a hundred million years and stop it, and gave a law for it to spin on a gravitational line and not to move from that gravitational line.

Then another clinker flew off the sun and it fell for millions of years and He stop it, and said stay there and spin on a gravitational line and do not move from that gravitational line. He created all of the planets in that order and gave them laws not to move from their gravitational line. He was writing His first Bible the zodiac with the stars. The earth was a big clinker that flew off the sun and became a big iceberg and down beneath it was nothing but burning volcano."

"The Son of God move the earth iceberg close to the sun and it starting melting and then great big glaciers begin to cut out the mountains and northern lands and the earth was covered with water. And the whole world was without form and void and water was upon the face of the deep." [Genesis 1:2]

The man clothed in linen said, "After the LORD God created the earth and the planets, He brought man down from the little sacred Halo of light to a little white cloud, and gave him the rulership over the earth." This little white cloud of Deity was put in Adam and not the animals." "Then the LORD God form man from the dust of the earth and breathe into His nostrils and man became a living soul. When Adam fell in sin that little white cloud in there became marred and blacken with sin and caused him to die and lose eternal life. Then the LORD God separated Adam's celestial body, "his soul"; from his spirit and his soul returned back to the hands of God because it was a part of God's eternal Spirit. The devil, Satan dirty hands could not take Adam's soul. [Genesis chapter 1:26-27].

The man clothed in linen said, "When the LORD God's redemption story and His plan of redemption is finish on earth, the saints souls and spirits will return to the earth

13

and will reunite with their redeemed earthly bodies and will rise from the graves, seas and from the ashes of the earth. After their souls and spirits are reunited with their earthy redeemed bodies they will be tranformed into glorified bodies to live with the Lord Jesus on earth in the golden city for Eternity." William asked the man clothed in linen, "What golden city?" The man clothed in linen said, "I will take you there and show it to you." William asked the man clothed in linen, "What is the different between the soul and the spirit, I don't understand?" The man clothed in linen said, "The different between the soul and the spirit, the soul of man is his Theophany, his celestial body that rotated off the great celestial Body of Jehovah God in the beginning. Adam's soul returned back to God after he sinned. The soul governs the actions of the spirit as the same as the natural brain controls the human body." William said, "I thought the soul and the spirit was one and the same."

The man clothed in linen said, "No, the soul can be separated from the spirit just as the spirit can be separated from the human body. Remember before Christ died on the cross, He said Father, into thy hands I commend my spirit, His Spirit separated from His body and ascended back to the Father, and His body went to the grave, and His Soul descended to hell in the lower regions of the earth, and He preached to the spirits that were in prison that repented not in the longsuffering of the days of Noah. " [Luke 23:46]

For Christ also hath once suffered for sins, the just for the unjust, that he might bring us to God, being put to death in the flesh, but quickened by the Spirit. By which also he went and preached unto the spirits in prison; Which sometime were disobedient, when once the longsuffering of God waited in the days of Noah, while the ark was a preparing, wherein few, that is, eight souls were saved by water. [1 Peter 3:18-20]

The man clothed in linen said, "the Lord Jesus soul also descended into Paradise that were in the lower regions of the earth where the old patriarchs were held. The antediluvian patriarchs Adam, Seth, Job, Noah and their wives, the other patriarchs after the flood, Abraham, Isaac, Jacob, Josheph, and others were held in a place called Paradise, separate from hell. That is why the Lord Jesus told the thief on the cross that he would be with Him in Paradise when the thief recognized that Jesus was the Son of God upon the cross. The Lord Jesus told a story of hell to the Pharisees who did not believe in his teaching." He stated: "There was a certain rich man, which was clothed in purple and fine linen, and fared sumptuously every day: And there was a certain beggar named Lazarus, which was laid at his gate, full of sores, And it came to pass, that the beggar died, and was carried by the angels into Abraham's bosom: the rich man also died, and was buried; And in hell he lift up his eyes, being in torments, and seeth Abraham afar off, and Lazarus in his bosom. And he cried and said, Father Abraham, have mercy on me, and send Lazarus, that he may dip the tip of his finger in water, and cool my tongue; for I am tormented in this flame. But Abraham said, Son, remember that thou in thy lifetime receivedst thy good things, and likewise Lazarus evil things: but now he is comforted, and thou art tormented." [Luke 16:19:31]

"The old patriarchs accepted the blood atonement under the blood of beasts but their spirits were still held in captivity in Paradise because the blood of lambs, bulls, and goats could not take away the stain of sin and redeem their souls from the right hand of God. They needed a kinsman redeemer to redeem their souls out of the right hand of God and their spirits from out of Paradise. The man clothed in linen opened the ancient scroll and read from Isaiah 61:1-3; The Spirit of the Lord is upon Me, because He has anointed Me to preach the gospel to the meek; He has sent Me to heal the brokenhearted, to proclaim liberty to the captives, and the opening of the prison to them that are bound; To proclaim the acceptable year of the LORD, and the day of vengeance of our God; to comfort all that mourn; To appoint unto them that mourn in Zion, to give unto them beauty for ashes, the oil of joy for mouring, the garment of praise for the spirit of heaviness; that they might be called trees of righteousness, the planting of the Lord, that he might be glorified.

Wherefore He saith, When He ascended up on high, he led captivity captive, and gave gifts unto men. (Now that he ascended, what is it but that he also descended first into the lower parts of the earth? He that descended is the same also that ascended up far above all heavens, that he might fill all things.) [Ephesians 4:8-10] When the Lord Jesus rose from the grave the old patriarchs spirits were delivered out of Paradise from captivity and their spirits were reuntied with their souls in the first resurrection. Their earthy bodies were resurrected from the graves and their Theophanies went into the holy city jerusalem and appeared unto many people and when they were seen, they vanished." [Matthew 27:53] When they ascended to heaven they told the Angels to lift up the gates and let the King of glory in." [Psalms 24:7-10]

The man clothed in linen said, "Lucifer has deceived numberous people on earth to disbelieve the Word of God that there is no burning hell, and that the scriptures contradicts each other and isn't true. The people are under Lucifer spell and have changed the truth of God's Word into a lie, and chose to worship nature and the creatures rather than the Creator. The LORD God can be seen in all of His Creation. Who gives the flowers its different colors, who painted the different colors on the salt water fishs, who tells the tree sap to go into its roots during the winter months and gives the tree resurrection power to come back to life in the spring time. The people are unaware that they are under the spell of the devil and will go to a burning hell if they reject Christ's salvation."

"The devil don't want people to know the truth that they will be held accountable for their sins and wickness on this earth. There is going to be a great white throne judgment for all sinners on earth who reject the Lord Jesus Christ blood sacrifice atonement." [Revelation 20:10-15] For we must all appear before the judgment seat of Christ; that every one may receive the things done in his body, according to that he hath done, whether it be good or bad. [2 Corinthians 5:10] The man clothed in linen said to William, "Now I will take you and show you the golden city that the Lord Jesus has built for His saints." They were translated through a portal to the seventh dimension and upon their arrival, William was astonish when he saw the beautiful transparent golden city that had the appearance of golden crystal. The walls around the city was made of pearls and other precious stones and the city streets and avenues was made of transparent gold. [Revelation 21:1-2,18-23]

After the man clothed in linen showed William the golden city, He said, "Now I am going to take you back to earth and show you where the ancient remedy to all diseases can be found." The dream scene changed and they were back on earth in the holy city of Jerusalem. The man clothed in linen said, "The remedy for all diseases is hidden under the temple mount inside a secret chamber." The man clothed in linen took William to a secret cave under the Temple mount. There were ancient scription and cherubims engraved on the walls. The man clothed in linen interpreted the ancient

18

scription on the walls and a secret passage opened and many torches inside lit automatically. The man clothed in linen said,

"We need to retrieve six ancient Tokens that are hidden in the cave walls in order to open the secret chamber where the cure to all diseases can be found. The six Tokens must be place in the wall grooves by the seven Token to open the secret chamber. They found and retrieved all six Tokens from out of the walls as they walked through several different passages in the cave, and came to a large under ground cistern that had six circular grooves in the cave wall. The man clothed in linen put all six Tokens inside of the six grooves by the seventh Token, and interpreted the ancient scription on all seven Tokens, and a secret chamber opened. The golden Ark of the Covenant was hidden inside the secret chamber and guarded by two Angels. The two Angels let the man clothed in linen opened the golden Ark of the Covenant and took two stone tablets and one ancient scroll made of animal skins. The man clothed in linen said to William, "The ancient scription written on the two stone tablets were engraved by the finger of God, and the ancient scroll was written by the Prophet Moses." He stated, "The prescription for all diseases and their origin can be found in the ancient scroll." He opened the ancient scroll and read the first three chapters.

After the man clothed in linen finished reading the first three chapters in the ancient scroll, He reiterated to

William, "The LORD God Almighty created the first man from His enternal Spirit in the beginning before any other creatures were created. Man is special because he is the only creature that were born with Deity, a soul from the living God and have rulership over the earth." "After the LORD God created all the sea creatures, birds and animals, He spoke to the dust of the earth and told the elements; oxygen, carbon, hydrogen, nitrogen, calcium, phosphorus, Potassium, Sodium, Chlorine, Magnesium, and Sulfur to come together to form man and the elements materialize, swirled around the Word of the living God and a man appeared out of the dust of the earth as a tree. The LORD God Spoke Adam's Theophany into the man and he became a living soul. William said to the man clothed in linen, "I thought the LORD God formed man from the dust of the earth." The man clothed in linen stated, "No", the LORD God do not use His hands to form anything, He just speaks His thoughts and the elements materialize around His Word and His thoughts are created." After He form the man from the dust of the earth He called Adam's Theophany into the earthy body.

By the sweat of your brow will you have food to eat until you return to the ground from which you were made. For you were made from dust, and to dust you will return. [NLTGenesis 3:19] The LORD God instructed His Son Adam that he could eat the fruits from all of the trees in the Garden, except from the tree of knowledge of good and evil.

He told Adam the tree of knowledge of good and evil was a tree of death, and if he eat from it, he will surely die. The LORD God saw that Adam was lonesome and said it was not good for him to be alone and put him asleep and took one of his ribs and created a woman. Adam told the woman they could eat the fruits from all the trees except from the tree of knowledge of good and evil."

"The woman went walking one day in the garden alone without Adam and came across the serpent. The serpent charmed the woman into eating the forbidden fruit from the tree of the knowledge of good and evil. She went and told Adam what she had done and Adam knew the woman was going to die because she had eaten from the forbidden fruit. Adam love the woman and did not want to see her die because she was created from his spirit and was bone of his bone and flesh of his flesh. Adam knew the LORD God was going to kill the woman because she had disobeyed His Word and had eaten from the tree of knowledge of good and evil."

"Adam decided to partake in the woman sin by eating from the tree of death and to die with the woman because she was a part of him. The man clothed in linen told William, "The Lord Jesus did the same thing that Adam did when He died for a sin offering for His elect children. He willfully took His children sins upon Him and gave His life for a blood sacrifice atonement to redeem His children back to eternal life because they were created from His Spirit and

Word in the beginning. After Adam and Eve had eaten the fruit from the tree of knowledge of good and evil, their eyes were open and they realized they were naked, and sewed fig leaves together and made aprons to cover their private parts. The LORD God came in the garden one evening to have fellowship with His children and they hid themselves in the bushes and trees. They disobeyed their Father and ate the forbidden fruit from the tree of knowledge of good and evil."

"The LORD God asked Adam who told you that you were naked? He said the woman gave the tree to me and I did eat. Then He asked the woman who told you that you were naked? She said the serpent charmed me into eating the fruit, and I ate from the tree of knowledge of good and evil. The LORD God would have killed them immediately but instead, He killed an innocent lamb and shed its blood as an atonement for their sins." "The LORD God took the little Lamb's bloody skins and cover His children nakedness because the fig leaves wasn't sufficient. The Lord Jesus did the same thing when the centurion Soldiers stripped Him naked and put Him upon the cross to die for our sins. The Lord Jesus willfully chose to die upon the cross naked as the Lamb of God for a sin offering for His children and to take away their shame." Looking unto Jesus the author and finisher of our faith; who for the joy that was set before him endured the cross, despising the shame, and is set down at the right hand of the throne of God. [Hebrews 12:2]

"The lamb's blood was only a temporarily remedy for the LORD God's law of death. The innocent animal blood could not take away the curse of death and could not redeem them back to eternal life because the LORD God had said if they eat from the tree of the knowledge of good and evil, they will surely die." "The LORD God's children could no longer have fellowship with Him and couldn't come in His Holy presence anymore because they had sinned and lost eternal life. They had to leave the garden and the LORD God placed Angels with flaming swords at the east gate of garden to keep His children from His Holy presence. William asked the man clothed in linen, "why did the Lord not forgive His children of their sins?" The man clothed in linen said, "if the LORD God would have foregiven His children of their sins all creation would have vanished because He had spoken all creation into existence by His Spoken Word, and if He would have taken back his Word of the curse of death, the whole earth would have turned back to atoms and molecules and cosmic light. Before the fall, Adam and Eve had dominion over the earth as a son and daughter of God. They could speak to nature and the elements of the earth and they would obey them. Adam had the abstract title deed to the earth and to eternal life within his Theophany, his soul, Word body because he was born from the eternal Spirit and the WORD of the LORD God Almighty. He was born with Deity and was an amateur god on earth. He could speak to nature and all the animals and they would obey him.

"He could tell a tree to move on the other side of the river and the tree would move to the other side of the river. He could tell it to rain and to stop raining. He could tell a mountain to move or to become a plain and immediately the mountain would be flatten to a plain. "As a son of God Adam had spoken WORD authority from his Father the LORD God Almighty. After Adam sinned, Lucifer could not take his Theophany because it went back to the right hand of the LORD God Almighty but his spirit remained marred in his earthly body and was now in the hands of the devil and was subjective to sickness and death. "Adam no longer had his Theophany and dominion to speak to nature and the elements of the earth because the LORD God had taken back his Theophany because it was a part of God's eternal life and the devil dirty hands could not take it."

"The woman was not created with a Theophany because she was taken from Adam's rib, "his feminine spirit" and was a byproduct of Adam but she had eternal life because she was created from him, as he was created from the LORD God Almighty. There was a price to pay to break the curse of sin and death, and to redeem God's elect children out of Book of Redemption. The Lord Jesus paid the price with His blood sacrifice atonement at Calvary and redeemed His children souls but their earthy bodies is subjective to sickness and death because Satan still have their earthy bodies under the control of sin and death, that is why human beings suffer with sickness and death. When the Lord Jesus return and take possession of His redemptive claims the saints earthy bodies will be lift from the curse of sin and death and will be change into glorified bodies."

"According as he hath chosen us in him before the foundation of the world, that we should be holy and without blame before him in love: Having predestinated us unto the adoption of children by Jesus Christ to himself, according to the good pleasure of his will, to the praise of the glory of his grace, wherein he hath made us accepted in the beloved. In whom we have redemption through his blood, the forgiveness of sins, according to the riches of his grace; Wherein he hath abounded toward us in all wisdom and prudence; Having made known unto us the mystery of his will, according to his good pleasure which he hath purposed in himself: That we should be to the praise of his glory, who first trusted in Christ. In whom ye also trusted, after that ye heard the word of truth, the gospel of your salvation: in whom also after that ye believed, ye were sealed with that Holy Spirit of promise, which is the earnest of our inheritance until the redemption of the purchased possession, unto the praise of his glory." [Ephesians 1:4-14]

"The Lord Jesus shed His blood and died on the cross at Calvary to redeem His elect children celestial bodies and their earthy bodies because the serpent, injected his gene into the bloodline of the human race when he subduced the woman to eat the forbidden fruit. This event will be describe in more detail in the "Serpent Seed" chapter."

CHAPTER 4

THE SERPENT SEED

After the man clothed in linen finished reading the first three chapters in the ancient scroll, he said to William, "Before the world was created the LORD God Almighty also created Angelic beings as He did with the sons of God. [Genesis 1:27] "The LORD God created a beautiful Angel and called his name Lucifer, son of the morning because his beauty shone like the sun. [Isaiah 45:7] He was a chosen instrument of God and was created with evil intentions to fulfill God's plan of redemption story. Lucifer was created with the most beautiful Angelic voice and his beauty and his Angelic voice caused him to be full of pride and he sinned against the sons of God by lying on them before God day and night." "And I heard a loud voice saying in heaven, now is come salvation, and strength, and the kingdom of our God, and the power of his Christ: for the accuser of our brethren is cast down, which accused them before our God day and night." [Revelation 12:10] "Lucifer wanted the other Angels to worship him instead of the LORD God Almighty and started a rebellion against the LORD God Almighty, the sons of God and the other Angels in heaven."

"How art thou fallen from heaven, O Lucifer, son of the morning! How art thou cut down to the ground, which didst weaken the nations! For thou hast said in thine heart, I will ascend into heaven, I will exalt my throne above the stars of God: I will sit also upon the mount of the congregation, in the sides of the north: I will ascend above the heights of the clouds; I will be like the most High." [Isaiah 14:12-14] "Lucifer deceived one third of the Angels to join him in his rebellion against the LORD God but they did not prevail. The LORD God placed a curse upon Lucifer for rebelling against Him and stripped him of his beauty, and cursed the Angels that participated with him in the rebellion." "The LORD God changed their angelic appearance to the appearance of demons and casted them out of heaven with chains of darkness into the bottomless pit but the LORD God permitted some of them to escape to fulfill His redemption story."

And his tail drew the third part of the stars of heaven, and did cast them to the earth. And there was war in heaven: Michael and his angels fought against the dragon; and the dragon fought and his angels, And prevailed not; neither was their place found any more in heaven. And the great dragon was cast out, the <u>old serpent</u>, <u>called the devil</u>, and Satan, which deceives the whole world: he was cast out into the earth, and his angels were cast out with him. [REVELATION 12:4,7,9]

"After the angelic war in heaven the devil, that old serpent was cast out of heaven into the earth. Lucifer's objective was to deceive the whole world and to cause the people of God to worship him, instead of the LORD God Almighty.""Therefore rejoice, ye heavens, and ye that dwell in them. Woe to the inhabiters of the earth and of the sea! for the devil is come down unto you, having great wrath, because he knoweth that he hath but a short time". [REVELATION 12:12]

The man clothed in linen said, "When the LORD God casted Lucifer that <u>old serpent,</u> out of heaven, he went and embodied a Beast that was in the midst of the garden of Eden, which was called the serpent, to deceive God's children Adam and Eve, and to cause them to sin against their Creator." [Ezekiel 28:13]. "The LORD God foreknew that Lucifer, that <u>old serpent</u> would enter into the Beast and charm the woman. That is why the LORD God had Moses to write the prophecy in Genesis 3:15; I will put enmity between the serpent seed and the woman seed, and that He, [Christ] would crush the old serpent head on the cross at Calvary." The reader may be thinking, no it was a serpent. I pray as the reader continue to read their eyes will be open to see it was a Beast and not a serpent.

The man clothed in linen said to William, "I am now going to reveal to you the mystery of what really happen in the Garden of Eden between the Beast and the woman. After the LORD God created the woman and brought her to Adam, he told her that the LORD had instructed him not to eat from the tree of the knowledge of good and evil, and if he eat from it, he will surely die. The tree of the knowledge of good and evil was a Beast in his original body form with arms and legs as a human being around 9 to 10 feet tall. He was more handsome than Adam, subtle and could reason and talk and the ancient Canaanites giants were his descendants." "The woman went walking in the garden one day alone without Adam and came across the Beast, he asked her in a subtle way has God said you shall not eat of every tree of the garden?"

"And the woman said we can eat of the fruit of the trees in the garden but of the fruit of the tree which is in the midst of the garden we cannot eat. God has said the day we eat, we will surely die. The Beast, which was called the old serpent lied to the woman and said you will not surely die if you eat the fruit from the tree of the knowledge of good and evil." "He lied and change one word, you will <u>NOT</u> surely die but the LORD God said you <u>WILL</u> surely die. The LORD God foreknew that the woman would be deceive by the Beast because she wasn't born with a Theophany like Adam and was the weaker vessel. The Beast deceived the woman by telling her that her eyes will be open to know good and evil as gods." [Genesis 3:1-7] [1 Peter 3:7] The man clothed in linen said, "The ancient writing in the scroll relating to the forbidden fruit that Adam and Eve ate is written symbolically. What really happen in the garden between the Beast and the woman, the Beast had a seed that could mingle with the woman, and Lucifer, that old serpent knew it, so he used the Beast body and charmed the woman into having sexual intercourse. The woman went and told Adam what she had done and that it was good, and had sex with Adam and their holy veils fell from their eyes and they discovered they were naked. "They sewed fig leaves together and covered their private parts." That is the reason scientists say human being evolved from apes but they will never find the missing link because the LORD God cursed the Beast and changed every bone in his body as a serpent to crawl upon the ground as a snake."

The man clothed in linen said, "The ancient scroll must be read with inspiration and divine revelation in between the lines, in order to see the clear picture because they are written in symbolic. When the LORD God commanded them not to eat from the tree of knowledge of good and evil, it was symbolic and not literally eating a fruit from off a tree. Eve did not eat a tangible fruit from the tree of the knowledge of good and evil but it was a sex act that took place between the Beast and Eve. This sex act between the

Beast and Eve has caused every disease and death in the human race and this was how the Beast injected his seed into the human race." Thereafter, the woman body became the "Tree of Death", every human being that were going to be born through a woman was going to die because the Beast gene had contaminated the "Original Spoken Word Seed", blood life of the son and daughter of God." "The Holy Scriptures says, all have sinned and come short of the glory of God, and there is none righteous, no not one and their throat is an open sepulcher; with their tongues they have used deceit; the poison of asps is under their lips." [Roman 3:12-13] "The LORD God never told Adam and Eve they were naked. He had covered their eyes with holy veils and they did not know that they were naked. It is common sense that eating a fruit will not cause them to realize they were naked. After this sex act took place, the LORD God came in the garden looking for Adam and called out to him and they hid themselves because they were afraid and knew that they were naked."

"When LORD God asked Adam who told you that you were naked? He passed the buck and said the woman gave it to me and I did eat. When the LORD God asked the woman, she said the serpent charmed me and I did eat." [GENESIS 3:9-13] The man clothed in linen reiterated and said, "The tree of knowledge of good and evil was a Beast and not a serpent. The Tree of Life in the Garden of Eden was the Lord Jesus Christ, He created all life. After the Beast had this sexual affair with the woman, the LORD God cursed him and took away his arms and legs and changed his body form to that of a "Serpent" and casted him to the ground." And the LORD God said unto the serpent, Because thou hast done this, thou art cursed above all cattle, and above every beast of the field; upon thy belly shalt thou go, and dust shalt thou eat all the days of thy life. [GENESIS 3:14]

"When the LORD God instructed them not to eat from the tree of knowledge of good and evil, He was referring to receiving the Beast lies into their heart. The Beast called the old serpent, the devil, lied to Eve and she received his lies into her heart and was seduced into having sex with the Beast. The word <u>eat</u> is used in Holy Scriptures symbolically to<u> receive in thine heart"</u>. Moreover he said to me, Son of man, eat that you find;<u> eat this roll</u>, and go speak to the house of Israel. So I opened my mouth, and He caused me to eat that roll. And He said to me, Son of man, cause your belly to eat, and fill your bowels with this roll that I give you. Then did I eat it; and it was in my mouth as honey for sweetness. [EZEKIEL 3:1-3]

"The LORD God made it clear in Ezekiel 3:10; eat was symbolic to<u> receive in thine heart.</u> Moreover he said unto me, Son of man, all my <u>words</u> that <u>I shall speak</u> unto thee <u>receive in thine heart</u>, and hear with thine ears. [EZEKIEL

3:10] "This is what the woman did in the Garden of Eden when the Beast charmed her and she received his lies into her heart and was seduced. The fallen Angel Lucifer have several names, Satan, the dragon, the old serpent, the devil.""Lucifer wanted to set up his own kingdom on earth and to produce his own children to be worship like the Most High God on earth, he knew the Beast had a seed that would mingle with the woman, so he use the Beast body and charmed the woman into a sexual affair with him to produce his own children through the daughter of God. After Eve had sex with the Beast, she went and had sex with Adam and was impregnated with two seeds at the same time, the Beast seed and Adam's seed. Eve gave birth to twins, Cain and Abel. Cain was the son of the Beast the wicked one, the old serpent, the devil, and was not the son of Adam". In fact, Cain is not listed in Adam's genealogy. Abel is not listed because Cain murder his step brother Abel because he was jealous of Abel's revelation that God required a blood sacrifice offering for their sins. Cain had the wrong revelation and offered fruits to the Lord and the LORD God rejected Cain's fruit offering and he got mad and killed his step brother Abel because he had the nature of his father the Beast." [Genesis 4:3-11].

He that committeth sin is of the devil; for the devil sinneth from the beginning. For this purpose the Son of God was manifested, that he might destroy the works of the devil. Whosoever is born of God doth not commit sin; for his seed remaineth in him: and he cannot sin, because he is born of God. In this the children of God are manifest, and the children of the devil: whosoever doeth not righteousness is not of God, neither he that loveth not his brother. For this is the message that ye heard from the beginning, that we should love one another. Not as Cain, who was of that wicked one, and slew his brother. And wherefore slew he him? Because his own works were evil, and his brother's righteous. [1 John 3:8-12] "When the Beast and the woman had sexual intercourse, the Beast mingled his seed into the human race. When the Beast crossed his seed with the woman seed it caused every disease, sickness and death in the human race and the Beast gene produced the Canaanite giants. The prophecy of the woman seed bruising the serpent head was Christ". And I will put enmity between thee and the woman, and between thy seed and her seed, it shall bruise thy head, and thou shalt bruise his heel. [Genesis 3:15]]

"The Lord Jesus Christ crushed the serpent / Beast head at Calvary with His blood sacrifice atonement for an offering for sins and obliterated the cure of sin and death. Although the Lord Jesus did not sin, He became sin to take away the curse of sin by hanging upon the cross". And ye know that he was manifested to take away our sins; and in him is no sin. [1 John 3:5] Christ hath redeemed us from the curse of the law, being made a curse for us: for it is written, Cursed is every one that hangeth on a tree. [Galatians 3:13] "If the believer accept Christ's atonement that He made upon the cross for sins and accept Him as their personal Lord and Saviour, they will be save and justified by faith and forgiven of their sins, even on their dying bed from the Coronavirus, just as the thief hanging on the cross. The Lord Jesus saved the thief on the cross when the thief said, "Lord remember me when you returned to your kingdom." "The thief sample prayer of faith on the cross in recognizing that Jesus is Lord saved him. The Scriptures says "He that heareth My Words and believeth on Him that sent Me, has everlasting Life." Verily, verily, I say unto you, He that heareth my word, and believeth on him that sent me, hath everlasting life, and shall not come into condemnation; but is passed from death unto life. [John 5:24]

CHAPTER 5

KINSMAN REDEEMER

The man clothed in linen said to William, "When Adam and Eve sinned they lost their fellowship with their Father the LORD God Almighty and had to leave the eastside of garden of Eden because they could not be in their Father Holy presence because they had sinned. They had lost the rights to the title deed to the earth and eternal life and was separated from their Father the LORD God Almighty and needed a saviour to redeem them back to eternal life. So He drove out the man; and He placed at the east of the garden of Eden Cherubims, and a flaming sword which turned every way, to keep the way of the Tree of Life. [Genesis 3:24]

"The mystery to Tree of Life that was in the Garden of Eden was the LORD God almighty, He alone is the Creator and the source of all life. The tree of knowledge of good and evil was the Beast [the old serpent; the devil, Lucifer].

Adam and Eve needed a kinsman redeemer who was sinless to redeem them back to the Tree of Life. According to God's law of death He required a Kinsman Redeemer to pay the price for their sins and that price was for the blood of their lives, and He had to be born through the human race. The LORD God substituted an innocent Beast life to die instead of the blood of their lives because it was the Beast blood that contaminated the blood of the daughter of God when the Beast had sex with Eve and injected his blood seed into the human race, which produced Cain. And surely your blood of your lives will I require; at the hand of every beast will I require it, and at the hand of man; at the hand of every man's brother will I require the life of Man. [Genesis 9:5]

The man clothed in linen said, "The blood of an innocent Beast was only a temporarily substitute for the penalty of death. The LORD God required a blood sacrifice from a kinsman redeemer who was blameless to redeem man from the curse of God's law of sin and death. "This kinsman redeemer had to be born from the human race that had never sinned. Adam could not meet the requirement of redemption because he had sinned himself. There wasn't anyone blameless to redeem them because all men and women were born through sexual desire God could not use an Angel to redeem them because humans are not kindred to the Angels. There had to be someone born in the human race through a woman that had never sinned."

"The only way that God could redeem back His law of death and eternal life to His children, He had to redeem it Himself by becoming a kinsman redeemer. He was born through the sinful bloodline of the human race but it was His Own created sinless Blood that paid the price for the curse of death and to redeem His children back to eternal life. The grace of God met this kinsman redeemer in the person of Lord Jesus Christ, through the virgin birth. The Lord Jesus Christ is God Almighty, Emmanuel." For the wages of sin is death, but the gift of God is eternal life through Jesus Christ our Lord. [Romans 6:23]

The man clothed in linen said "Jesus is God." "He was neither the second person nor the third person, but He was God Almighty, Emmanuel in the flesh. He changed His stream from the Almighty to be a man to take on the form of man, so He could die to redeem man. He could not bleed in His Spirit body, so He created Himself a human body in Mary with His Own creative Blood Seed. Satan did not know the Creator was going to be born through the sinful bloodline of the human race to die as a kinsman redeemer. When the Lord Jesus died on the cross, He redeemed his own law of death from off of His children by paying the price with His Own sinless Blood and redeemed back His children to eternal life."

The man clothed in linen said, "when Satan had Christ crucified on the cross at Calvary, he did not know the law of death had no effect on Christ and could not keep Him in the grave because He is the Creator, the resurrection, and life." Jesus said unto her, I am the resurrection, and life: he that believeth in me, though he were dead, yet shall he live: And whoever liveth and believeth in me shall never die. Believeth thou this? [John 11:25]

For God so loved the world, that He gave His only begotten Son, that whosoever believes in Him should not perish, but have everlasting Life. [John 3:16] "The Lord Jesus Christ is our kinsman redeemer, He shed His precious blood at Calvary for a sacrificial atonement for a sin offering. He is the only mediator between God and men. The Lord Jesus made a new covenant with His Blood atonement that speaks better things than that of Abel." [1 Timothy 2:5] [Hebrew 12:24]. The man clothed in linen said, "Jehovah-jireh of the Old Testament is the Lord Jesus Christ of the New Testament. The Lord Jesus Christ is the LORD God Almighty. It was the Lord Jesus in the form of the pillar of cloud by day and the pillar of fire by night leading the children of Israel out of Egypt. He was the Angel of the Covenant, Christ did not come down to make Himself known, He came to reveal and make known the Father, He never talked about two Gods. Jehovah God did not have a physical body in the old Testament, He appeared to Moses as the Angel of the Covenant in the burning bush. When Moses asked to see Jehovah face, He said no man can see my face and live. Jehovah God told Moses that He would let him see the image of His back but not His face. Moses saw the back of Jehovah's Theophany. He appeared to the people in Old Testament as a Theophany but He did not have a flesh body until He was born in His Son Christ Jesus. When Jehovah God led the children of Israel out of Egypt, He was in the form of a pillar of fire. Although Jehovah God sent His Angels that appeared as men but no one had ever saw Jehovah face until Jesus Christ was born." [John 1:18] No man hath seen God at any time; the only begotten Son, which is in the bosom of the Father, He hath declared Him.

The man clothed in linen said, "The Lord Jesus is the High Priest that is clothed in the pillar of fire cloud garment down to His feet and with the golden girdle around His waist in the picture. The Prophet Ezekiel saw Him in his vision as seen in the picture." Then I beheld, and lo a likeness as the appearance of his loins even downward, fire; and from his loins even upward, as the appearance of brightness, as the color of amber. [Ezekiel Chapter 8:2] Who is the image of the invisible God, the firstborn of every creature: For by Him were all things created, that are in heaven, and that are in earth, visible and invisible, whether they be thrones, or dominions, or principalities, or powers: all things were created by Him, and for Him: and He is before all things, and by Him all things consist. [Colossian 1:15-17]"It was the Lord Jesus who said, I am the LORD and beside me there is no Saviour." [Isaiah 43:11].

"The Lord Jesus is the only Saviour and redeemer, He is the LORD Almighty that formed you from your mother's womb and created the heavens and the earth. He is the living God that makes all things. The LORD God said, "Look unto Me, and be ye saved, for I AM God, and there is none else." "Thou shalt know no God but Me; for there is NO SAVIOUR BESIDE ME." [Isaiah 44:24 / 45:22] The man clothed in linen said, "In the beginning before there ever was a star, a moon, or a galaxy, this great fountain of eternal Spirit had attributes that He wanted to express. Abraham called Him LORD God Almighty, Yahweh, Elohim the living God, He had eternal thoughts and attributes that He wanted to express and manifest for His own pleasure and glorification. He hath seen all things from the beginning to the ending because He is infinite and all knowing. Elohim wanted to be God but before He could be called God, He needed to have creatures to worship Him. The word "God" means "an object of worship". "There wasn't anyone to worship Him, so He created the Angels and they proclaimed Him God Almighty and worshipped Him. Elohim also wanted to be a Father and have sons and daughters, so He created them from His eternal Spirit in the beginning as immortal celestial heavenly beings and called <u>their name</u> Adam." [Genesis 5:1-2].

"Elohim wanted to become a Saviour but there wasn't anyone to save. There has to be a fallen entity first before He could ever display his attributes as a Saviour." The man clothed in linen said, "When Elohim created the earth in the beginning there wasn't a flesh man to till the ground because Adam was created a Theophany and walked in the garden as a celestial being. In order for Elohim to carry out His plan of redemption, He had to create flesh bodies for His sons and daughters and put them on free moral agency for they could choose right from wrong, in order for them to fall in sin for His plan of redemption to be fulfill." For the creature was made subject to vanity, not willingly, but by reason of him who hath subjected the same in hope, Because the creature itself also shall be delivered from the bondage of corruption into the glorious liberty of the children of God. [Romans 8:20-21]

"Elohim hath foreseen the fall of man and He permitted man to fall from grace in order for God to fulfill His majestic plan of saving them. Elohim prepared the solution for their sins even before the foundation of the world." [Revelation 13:8] tells us that the "Lamb was slain "before" the foundation of the world" to act as an atonement for sin. The LORD God wrote His elect children names in His book of redemption even before man could ever commit sin. Christ came to redeem His predestinated children not the children of Lucifer the devil."

For the children being not yet born, neither having done any good or evil, that the purpose of God according to election might stand, not of works, but of him that calleth; It was said unto her, the elder shall serve the younger. As it is written, Jacob have I loved, but Esau have I hated. What shall we say then? Is there unrighteousness with God? God forbid. For he saith to Moses, I will have mercy on whom I will have mercy, and I will have compassion on whom I will have compassion. For the scripture saith unto Pharaoh, Even for this same purpose have I raised thee up, that I might shew my power in thee, and that my name might be declared throughout all the earth. [Romans 9:11-17] "The above scriptures may seem cruel but Pharaoh was also a descendant of the Beast / serpent as Cain was, that is the reason he wore a serpent on his hat and had the people to worship him as God on earth. It was the LORD God's purpose to permit His children to fall in sin and to suffer sickness and death, it's all a part of His redemption story."

For I reckon that the sufferings of this present time are not worthy to be compared with the glory which shall be revealed in us. [Romans 8:18] "Elohim wanted to be a Healer too but how can He be a Healer if nobody got sick? There has to be sickness first before He could be a Healer. "Sickness and afflictions are part of God's permissive will to man in order to show and manifest to mankind His attributes of being a Healer." Psalms 103:2-3 states, *"Bless the LORD, O my soul, and forget not all his benefits: who forgiveth all thine iniquities; who healeth ALL thy diseases."*

"Consider the woman with the blood issue in Luke 8, she had a discharge of blood for twelve years and had spent all of her money on physicians that could not heal her." "This little woman saw that she couldn't get close to Jesus and said within herself, "if I can only touch the border of His garment, I'll be healed. She crawled on the ground under people until she was able to touch the border of His garment and immediately she felt her discharging stop. Jesus stopped and said "who touched me?" His disciples rebuked Him and said "Master, what are You talking about"? There are multitudes of people climbing over one another touching you. Jesus said, "but I perceive that I have gotten weak." "Virtue has gone from me." "Jesus look around and saw the little woman who had touched Him and said, "daughter be not afraid, your faith has healed you, go in peace." [Luke 8:41-48] "The little woman with the blood issue touched Him with a different kind of touch. This story of the woman with the blood issue just declared the glory and healing power of God and served as a testimonial of God's grace through each generation. Elohim also wanted to manifest Himself as a King, as a Priest, and as a Judge. So there has to be a kingdom set-up, a holy tabernacle set-up, and a judgment bar set up. These are His eternal thoughts and intentions before the foundation of the world, to get glory unto Himself."

The man clothed in linen said, "The LORD God knew that as a Spirit He will never be able to fulfill these plans without having a "body" that will act out His plans." "For example, it is written in His Law that *Almost all things are by the Law purged with blood; and without the shedding of blood is no remission*" [Hebrews 9:22]. Redemption requires death, Christ became our high priest and offer Himself as a sin offering and shed His blood for a new testament, that by means of His death, for the redemption of sins that were under the first testament. For where a testament is, there must also necessity be the death of the testator. [Hebrews 9:16].

"A Spirit cannot bleed and die, it takes BLOOD, therefore, to pay the penalty for sin Christ had to die. No Angel blood, no priest, no animal's blood, was ever worthy

45

to redeem man in his fallen estate." "That is the reason God had to be born in Christ and had to do it Himself, for there is no Saviour but Him alone. The Lord Jesus Christ had to do it in order to show that He alone is the ONLY Redeemer." In Isaiah 45:22, God said, "*Look unto Me, and be ye saved, for I AM God, and there is none else.*" "*Thou shalt know no God but Me; for there is NO SAVIOUR BESIDE ME*" (Hosea 13:4). Christ is the only Saviour there is. The key to the whole mystery of the Godhead is this. Jehovah God knew that He, as God, could not die and bleed in the Spirit, for a Spirit has no flesh and bones. His own law required blood for an atonement. In order for God to fulfill His master plan of redeeming mankind, He had to put on a <u>veil of flesh</u>, in order to taste death and <u>pay the penalty for His Own law of death</u>, to justify His children from the curse of sin." That is to fulfill Romans 3:28, "*Therefore we conclude that a man is justified by faith without the deeds of the law.*" "*For by grace are ye saved through faith; and that not of yourselves: it is the gift of God: not of works, lest any man should boast*" [Ephesians.2:8,9]. The man clothed in linen said, "All of nature, the trees, flowers, grass, animals, birds, are groaning and travailing for the sons of God to be delivered for the curse of sin and death because they will be delivered from the curse also. The grass of the fields want to be delivered from the curse when the LORD God cursed the ground to bear weeds, thorns and thistles. [Genesis 3:17]. "Christ has already redeemed us from the curse and paid the price for sin and death with His Own Blood but He hasn't claim and taken possession yet."

For we know that the whole creation groaneth and travaileth in pain together until now. And not only they, but ourselves also, which have the first fruits of the Spirit, even we ourselves groan within ourselves, waiting for the adoption, to wit, the redemption of our body. [Romans 8:22-23] "When the last elect child of God accept His blood sacrifice atonement, Christ will come and take possession of His redeemed children from the earth and pour out His wrath on the ungodly." The man clothed in linen said, "Jesus is the Lamb, who was slain and is the One setting upon the throne of God with the Book of Redemption that is sealed with seven seals in His right hand, making intercession as a Mediator between God and man with His Blood on the mercy seat. He will come forth with the Book of Redemption that holds the secret to plan of redemption when the last elect child of God accept His Blood sacrifice atonement. After Adam and Eve sinned Christ took the title deed to the earth and eternal life and sealed the Book of Redemption with seven seals. No man in heaven, nor on earth, neither under the earth was found worthy to pay the price of redemption. The Angels could not redeem the Book of Redemption because they are not kindred to the humans."

The man clothed in linen said, "Christ is the Lion and Lamb, which is, and which was, and which is to come, the Almighty. He along was worthy to redeem the Book of Redemption. John saw a Lamb come forth to take the Book and it look like it had been slain and was wounded, cut and bruised, and bleeding. It was Christ way back into the Eternities making intercession with His blood as a Mediator between God and man, showing that those who had come to God under the offering of the blood of beasts for a substitutionary offering." The man clothed in linen said, "When Christ intercession as a Mediator between God and man is finish, He will come forth not as a Lamb but the Lion of the tribe of Juda and claim His redemptive saints and pour out His wrath upon the earth on those people who rejected His Blood sacrifice atonement." [Revelation 5:1-14] [Revelation 8:1-13]

CHAPTER 6

THE ANGEL OF DEATH

The LORD is my shepherd; I shall not want. He maketh me to lie down in green pastures: he leadeth me beside the still waters. He restoreth my soul: he leadeth me in the paths of righteousness for his name's sake. Yea, thought I walk through the valley of the shadow of death, I will fear no evil: for thou art with me; thy rod and thy staff they comfort me. Thou preparest a table before me in the presence of mine enemies: thou anointest my head with oil; my cup runneth over. Surely goodness and mercy shall follow me all the days of my life: and I will dwell in the house of the LORD forever. [Psalm 23:1-23] "The death Angel is sweeping the world with the COVID-19 pandemic and thousands of people has lose their lives. Over 1,900 years ago the Lord Jesus rose from the dead and gave the world a prescription for every disease and sickness. In order for the prescription to work the people must accept the Lord Jesus Christ sacrificial blood atonement. There's a blood atonement on God's altar in heaven for Divine healing for the COVID-19 virus but it will never do any good until the people confess their sins and accept the Lord Jesus Christ as their Lord and Saviour."

"The Coronavirus plague outbreak parallel with a Biblical event that happen over 3,000 years ago when an ancient plague struck the land of Egypt and killed all the first born children and all the firstborn cattle. In Exodus Chapter 12 the LORD God instructed Moses to tell the people to take a lamb without blemish in the (10) day of the month and keep it for fourteen (14) days in the same month and then kill the lamb in the evening on the 14 day. The people had to take the blood and put it upon the side door posts and the upper door post of their houses." "The LORD God said the blood would be for a token upon the house and when He saw the blood, the judgment plague would pass over that house, and would not kill the first born. After the LORD God delivered the children of Israel out of the land of Egypt from their taskmasters, He did not lead them to the promise land because He said the people would be afraid when they saw war and would return to Egypt, so He led them through the way of the wilderness by the red sea." [Exodus 13:17]

"The LORD God hardened Pharaoh's heart to pursue after the children of Israel. He wanted to demonstrate His mighty power before the children of Israel and before the Egyptians. The people thought they was going straight to the promise land. They did not know that the Lord God was leading them to the red sea to demonstrate His mighty power. The LORD led the children of Israel by a pillar of cloud by day and a pillar of fire by night to give them light. When they arrived at the red sea and saw the Egyptians pursing after them they started complaining to Moses and said there wasn't enough graves in Egypt, why did you bring us out here in the wilderness to die. They did not know that the LORD God was going to fight the Egyptians army for them by drowning them in the red sea. The LORD God caused a strong wind to blow on the sea all night and made the water to divide like a wall on both sides and the people went cross on dry land."

"The Egyptian pursued after them with chariots in the midst of the sea and the LORD God took off the chariots wheels to slow the Egyptians pursue. The LORD God told Moses to stretch forth his hand over the sea for the waters to return to drown the Egyptians. Moses stretched forth his hand over the sea and the waters covered the chariots and drowned all the Egyptians army in the midst of the sea." "The children of Israel saw that the waters had destroyed all of the Egyptians soldiers and then the people worshiped and feared the LORD God. When the children of Israel arrived in the wilderness, their hungry pains made them started complaining again to Moses that he had brought them to the wilderness to die of starvation." [Exodus 14:5-31] "The people had quickly forgotten about how the LORD God had delivered them from the Egyptians and destroyed Pharaoh Soldiers in the sea. They had forgotten that the LORD God was amongst them and leading them by His Angel of the Covenant in the form of a pillar of cloud by day and a pillar of fire by night to give them light. The man clothed in linen said, "The people have done the same thing today they have forgotten about the LORD God and have turned to idols even in the midst of the Covid-19 pandemic."

"The LORD God stated, if My people who are called by My name, will humble themselves, and pray and seek My face, and turn from their wicked ways, then I will answer, and will forgive their sin, and will heal their land." [2 Chronicles 7:14]. "The LORD God's elect people don't have to fear the COVID-19 virus because He is the LORD of the dead and the living and have the keys of Hell and Death. He have ALL power to heal His people from any disease or sickness but they must trust in Him. If they need healing and food, He will provide, HE is Jehovah-jireh. He provided food and water for over two (2) million Israelites in the wilderness, and He will provide for His chosen people today in this pandemic. When the children of Israel needed meat, He caused a wind to blow from the sea and brought quails from everywhere and they gather them up and had meat to eat." "They didn't even have to hunt for them. The LORD God Almighty created the quails and made water come from out of a rock in the wilderness, and He rained down bread (manna) from heaven to feed them. He is still

Jehovah-jireh, the LORD will provide for His people. When the people got thirsty and did not have any water to drink in the wilderness, He gave them water from the rock. When they got sick, He provided healing for them and there wasn't any hospitals in the wilderness nor did they have pharmacies to get medication." "The world is in a neurotic state due to the COVID-19 virus but there is Divine healing in the Blood of the Lord Jesus Christ. He was the rock in the wilderness that provided water for people and the Bread that rained down from heaven and the quails that blew in from the sea. He is Jehovah-jireh, the Creator of all things."

Come unto me, all ye that labour and are heavy laden, and I will give you rest. Take my yoke upon you, and learn of me; for I am meek and lowly in heart: and ye shall find rest unto your souls. [Matthew 11:28] There are two amazing miracles recorded in the Holy Scriptures when the Lord Jesus feed 5,000 and 4,000 people on two different occasions, and there wasn't any grocery stores in the wilderness. He is still Jehovah-jireh, "the LORD will provide." The Lord Jesus took five loaves of bread and two fish and blessed them and broke them into pieces and instructed His disciples to give them to the people and all 5,000 people ate and there were twelve basketfuls of broken pieces that were left over. On another occasion He took seven loaves and two fish and broke them into pieces and instructed His disciples to give them to the people and all 4,000 people ate and there were seven basketfuls of broken pieces that were left over. Matthew 14:14-21 / 5:29-39]

The Lord Jesus Christ is Jehovah-jireh, He will provide for His people in a time of famine. People who place their faith and trust in Him, He will heal them and provide all of their needs. Who forgiveth all thine iniquities; who health all thy diseases." [PSALMS 103:3] The Lord Jesus is the Great Physician that health all diseases but people must look to Him and place their faith in Him for their healing. The Lord Jesus can heal people who are infected with the Coronavirus. They must place total faith in Him for their healing and don't doubt in their heart, if they want to be heal."And he arose out of the synagogue, and entered into Simon's house. And Simon's wife's mother was taken with a great fever; and they besought him for her. And he stood over her, and rebuked the fever; and it left her; and immediately she arose and ministered unto them. Now when the sun was setting, all they that had any sick with divers diseases brought them unto him; and he laid his hands on every one of them, and healed them. [Luke 4:38, 39] The Lord Jesus is the same yesterday, today, and forever, and His blood atonement not only cleanses us of sins but from all sickness and diseases but we must accept His blood atonement by faith for our sins and sickness."Jesus Christ the same yesterday, and today, and forever. [Hebrews 13:8]

CHAPTER 7

THE BRASS SERPENT ON THE POLE

The man clothed in linen told William, "The brass signifies judgment and the brazen serpent on the pole symbolize the original sin of the serpent in the Garden of Eden when the Beast / serpent charmed Eve and caused her to sin. The brass serpent further symbolized that God was going to put Divine judgment on Christ for the sins of the world. The LORD God had to break the curse of sin and death by placing Divine judgment upon His Son Jesus Christ for an offering for sins. He paid the price of redemption with His Own blood at Calvary."

"When the LORD God deliver the children of Israel out of Egypt from bondage they started complaining against Moses for bringing them into the wilderness to die because there wasn't any water and no place to grow food.

The LORD God sent venomous snakes into their camp to kill them for their sins. The serpents started biting and killing thousands of people and they cried out to Moses and asked him to pray to God to take away the serpents. Moses interceded and prayed for the people and the LORD God instructed Moses to make a brass serpent and put it upon a pole." And the people spake against God, and against Moses, Wherefore have ye brought us up out of Egypt to die in the wilderness? for there is no bread, neither is there any water; and our soul loatheth this light bread. And the LORD sent fiery serpent among the people, and they bit the people; and much people of Israel died. Therefore the people came to Moses, and said, We have sinned, for we have spoken against the LORD, and against thee; pray unto the LORD, that he take away the serpents from us. And Moses prayed for the people. [Numbers 21:5-7]

And the Lord said to Moses, make you a fiery serpent, and set it upon a pole: and it shall come to pass, that every one that is bitten, when he looks upon it, shall live. And Moses made a serpent of brass, and put it upon a pole, and it came to pass, that if a serpent had bitten any man, when he beheld the serpent of brass, he lived. [Number 21:8-9]

"The people had to look at the serpent on the pole when they were bitten by a serpent if they wanted to be heal. The LORD God did not take away the serpents from the people but made an atonement for their sins. The people had to be obedient to the Prophet Moses and had to look upon the brass serpent on the pole with faith and without fear, if they wanted to live. This same principle applies today, the people must look to the Lord Jesus Christ sacrificial blood atonement with faith, if they want to be heal from any disease and to receive eternal life." "The Lord Jesus typed the brass serpent upon the pole when the LORD God placed divine judgment upon Him at Calvary for a sacrificial Blood atonement for the people sins. The Lord Jesus has obliterated sin, and has broken off the stinger of death at Calvary. Christ the sinless One, became sin for us so that we can be called righteous. Our sins was placed upon Him and He willfully gave up His life for a sin offering for us, to redeem back God's law of death that we might be made the righteousness of God in Him." For he hath made him to be sin for us, who knew no sin; that we might be made the righteousness of God in him. [2 Corinthians 5:21] O death, where is thy sting? O grave, where is thy victory? The sting of death is sin; and the strength of sin is the law. But thanks be to God, which giveth us the victory through our Lord Jesus Christ. [1Corinthians 15:55-57]

"The LORD God had already foreordained judgment on His Son Christ Jesus before there were any sinners. Salvation being entirely of the Lord, He trod the wine press of the fierceness of the wrath of God alone. His vestures were dyed crimson with His own blood. The fiery furnace of the just judgment and wrath of God was His portion." "He suffered, the just for the unjust. Thou art worthy, O Lamb of God, for Thou hast redeemed us by Thine own blood". He was wounded for our transgressions, He was bruised for our iniquities, the chastisement of our peace was upon him; and with his stripes we are healed." "The LORD hath laid upon Him the iniquity of us all. He stood the test of the fiery furnace, a test that no other one has gone through. He was made flesh in order to take upon Himself the judgments of God for sin. He suffered as no man had ever suffered. Even before the cross, He had shed great drops of sweat like blood from His body as in the intense agony of the ordeal ahead the very blood separated in His veins." [John 3:14,15] And as Moses lifted up the serpent in the wilderness, even so must the Son of man be lifted up: That whosoever believes in Him should not perish, but have eternal life

"The LORD God Almighty was made flesh in His Son Jesus by the virgin birth with His Own creative sinless Blood, and died at Calvary to pay the penalty of death for an atonement for the curse of sins. There could not have been a greater or more perfect sacrifice than God Himself becoming the Atonement Himself." And having made peace through the Blood of His cross, by Him to reconcile all things to Himself; by Him, I say, whether they be things in earth, or things in heaven. [Colossians 1:20] "The LORD God was manifested in flesh when He was born in His Son

Jesus through a woman; without any resulting sexual act but it was God Himself making both hemoglobin and egg cells in the womb of Mary, God Himself taking the form of a man in Jesus Christ, which was the FLESH of God, none other than God Himself creating a body of His own." And without controversy great is the mystery of godliness: <u>God</u> was manifest in the <u>flesh</u>, justified in the Spirit, seen of angels, preached unto the Gentiles, believed on in the world, received up into Glory. [First Timothy 3:16]

"The LORD God was in Christ reconciling the world unto himself, not imputing the trespasses unto them and has committed unto them the word of reconciliation. All have sinned, and come short of the glory of God and have forgotten about their Creator and went astray to worship idolatry and themselves. The people have forgotten that the LORD God created all the planets and placed them into the universe by His Spoken WORD. He is before all things, and in Him all things hold together." [Colossians 1:16-17]

"The LORD God doesn't want His elect people to be afraid of anything!" "He is in control and hold all things together. He created the worlds by His Spoken WORD and placed them in space spinning on invisible axles. He created the Sun and placed it in orbit and said stay there and don't come near the earth to burn it up. He ordered the comets and asteroids the size of mountains not to strike the earth until He have save all of His elect people, and have secretly taken them from the earth. He will pour out His wrath upon the earth when His redemption story is finished. He is the One that ordered the stars to stay in orbit and not to fall to earth. He is the One that gives Orders to the wind and the waves of the sea and they obey Him. He is the One that created oxygen for people to breathe on earth and did not create oxygen on any other planet. He is the One that Ordered gravity to hold all things together and all the planets in orbit around the Sun. He is the Holy One, the LORD God Almighty!"

CHAPTER 8

THE BLOOD TOKEN

When the man clothed in linen finished reading and explaining the ancient scroll to William, He stated, "all germ diseases starts in the blood stream and feeds off the Blood because the life is in the Blood." The man clothed in linen asked William, "Do you remember what was stated in the ancient scroll in Genesis 9:5?" He reiterated to William, "In the ancient times the LORD God required a lamb's blood to be put on the two side posts and on the upper door post of the house for the plague of death to pass over that house. The lamb's blood was for a Token to show the death Angel that death had already occurred in that house. When the death Angel saw the lamb's blood on the two side posts and on the upper door post, it met the requirement of God's judgment of death and the death Angel had to pass over that house."

The man clothed in linen opened the scroll and started reading from: [Genesis 9:5] And surely your blood of your lives will I require; at the hand of every beast will I require it, and at the hand of man; at the hand of every man's brother will I require the life of Man. "When Adam and Eve sinned in the beginning the LORD God required the blood of their lives but He substituted an innocent Beast life instead of their lives. The blood of a Beast substituted for the blood of their lives. That is why the LORD God rejected Cain's fruit offering for his sins, and accepted Abel's blood offering because it wasn't an apple, peach, pomegranate or an apricot as some people thinks but it was a sex act that contaminated the blood. "In the ancient times the worshipper had to apply the blood over himself and it showed that he had identified himself with the blood sacrifice of the Beast. The blood stood for a Token that the Beast life had died in place of the worshipper but the Beast blood could not take away their sins, it was only a temporarily covering for their sins.""The believer today must place their faith in the shed blood of Christ to be identified with His sacrifice and be born again of water and of the Spirit for the remission of sins. When the believer accept Christ as their Lord and Saviour and is baptized with water in His Name, they will receive the Holy Spirit and the new birth." [John 3:1-36]. "The Lord Jesus Christ was the perfect Lamb that shed His blood at Calvary for a sacrifice for the sins of the people. In ancient Egypt the blood had to be applied before the plague passed through the land. The people had to apply the blood by faith believing the wrath of God was going to smite the land of Egypt with the plague as Moses had said. They could not apply the blood after the plague had swept through the land of Egypt, it would have been too late."

"The blood identified that the worshipper had killed the lamb and had applied its blood as a Token upon the house for the death Angel to pass. Today in this modern time 2020, *the Holy Spirit in the believer is the blood Token* and not the Blood on the door posts of the house. *The Holy Spirit is the Token that God requires for the believer today. It is the literal Life of Jesus Christ, returned back into the believer.* If the believer have the Holy Spirit, its God's Token for today and the wrath of God's judgment will pass because Christ has already been judged."[Matthew 26:26-28] And as they were eating, Jesus took bread, and blessed it, and brake it, and gave it to the disciples, and said, Take, eat; this is my body. And he took the cup, and gave thanks, and gave it to them, saying, Drink ye all of it; For this is my blood of the new testament, which is shed for many for the remission of sins. Christ body is the Word and His Blood is Spirit]

"The chemistry of the blood of Jesus Christ that was shed at Calvary for the remission of sins has changed back to His eternal Spirit, Christ Words are Spirit and life. The believer must accept the Words of Christ by faith and feed on His Words and accept His Blood; Spirit to have eternal life."

"The believer must place their faith in the blood of Christ sacrificial atonement and be baptized in His name for the remission of sins, and they shall receive the blood Token, which is the Holy Spirit. This is the prescription for the forgiveness of sins and all diseases. In order for the believer to be identified with Jesus Christ death, burial and resurrection, they must be baptized into His name. It is critical that the believer be baptized in the name of the Jesus Christ to be identified with Him for the remission of sins. Then Peter said to them, Repent, and be baptized every one of you in the Name of JESUS CHRIST for the REMISSION OF SINS, and you SHALL receive the gift of the HOLY GHOST. [ACTS 2:38]

"If the believer has been baptized in the name of the Father and of the Son and of the Holy Ghost, that is not the correct formula for water baptism and for remission of sins. The apostles knew what the Lord Jesus meant when He said baptized in the name of the Father and of the Son and of the Holy Ghost. The apostles knew those were titles to the name of the Lord Jesus Christ. They knew the correct formula for water baptism and there is not place in scripture where they baptized any other way but in the name of the Lord Jesus Christ. The scripture clearly shows Paul found John disciples that weren't baptized in Christ name. He asked them did they receive the Holy Ghost since they believed. They said they were not told whether there is any

Holy Ghost. Then Paul asked them, how were you baptized? They said under John baptism. Then Paul told them that John baptized with the baptism of repentance and that they needed to be baptized over again in the Name of the Lord Jesus Christ. [ACTS 19:1-6]

For ye are all the children of God by faith in Christ Jesus. For as many of you as have been baptized into Christ have put on Christ. There is neither Jew nor Greek, there is neither bond nor free, there is neither male nor female: for ye are all one in Christ Jesus. And if ye be Christ's, then are ye Abraham's seed, and heirs according to the promise. [GALATIANS 26-29]

"If Jesus is "Both" Lord and Christ, then He (Jesus) is, and cannot be else but "Father, Son, and Holy Ghost" in ONE Person manifested in the flesh. It is NOT "God in three persons, blessed trinity," but ONE GOD, ONE PERSON with three major titles, with three offices manifesting those titles. Hear it once more. This same Jesus is "BOTH Lord and Christ." Lord (Father) and Christ (Holy Spirit) is Jesus, for HE (Jesus) is BOTH of them (Lord and Christ), which is: [Father - LORD] [Son - Jesus] [Holy Ghost - Christ] LORD JESUS CHRIST." For unto you is born this day in the city of David a Saviour, which is Christ the Lord. He was born the Christ, and eight days later when he was circumcised He was named Jesus, even as the Angel had told them. Yes, if there were three Gods, you might very well baptize for a Father, and a Son, and a Holy Ghost. But the REVELATION GIVEN TO JOHN was that there is ONE GOD and His Name is LORD JESUS CHRIST, and you baptize for ONE God and only one. That is why Peter baptized the way he did at Pentecost. He had to be true to the revelation which was, "Let all the house of Israel know assuredly, that God hath made that SAME JESUS, Whom ye have crucified, BOTH LORD AND CHRIST." [LUKE 2:11]

When the man clothed in linen finished reading the ancient scroll to William, He vanished, and William said, "I know what the cure to all diseases and sickness is, its faith in the Blood of the Lord Jesus Christ." "The believer must accept Christ's blood atonement for Divine Healing and place their faith in Him. This is the prescription that must be applied for all generations. The Lord Jesus Christ, Divine healing can cure: Coronavirus, Cancer, Diabetes, Heart Trouble, AIDS, and all other diseases and sickness, but the believer must place total faith in His blood atonement." **And the blood of Jesus Christ his Son cleanseth us from all sin [1 John 1:7].**

Just as the blood of Jesus Christ can cleanse of all sin, it can cleanse of all diseases and sickness.

With His stripes we are healed [Isaiah 53:5].

Oh, how I love Him
How I adore Him
My breath, my sunshine
My all in all,
The great Creator
Became my Savior
And all God's Fullness
Dwelleth in Him.

Without reluctance
Flesh and blood His substance,
He took the form of man
Revealed the hidden plan
Oh, glorious myst'ry
Sacrifice of Calv'ry
And now I know Thou wert the great *"I am"*

Printed in the United States
By Bookmasters